BR
f

GW00514763

the guidebook that pays for itself in one day

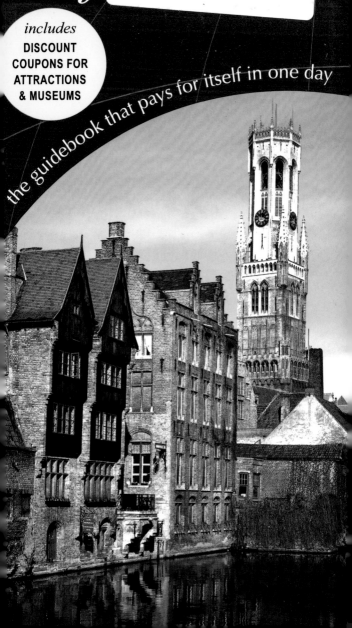

The *for less* Guidebook series...

- 288-page guidebooks
- Detailed fold-out street maps
- Discount card that gives up to 4 people great savings at 300 of the city's best places *(attractions, museums, restaurants, shops, tours etc).*

The *for less* Compact Guide series...

- 76-page guidebooks
- Detailed fold-out street maps
- 2-for-1 (or 50%) discounts at top attractions and museums

...PLUS 50 more for less Compact Guides to follow

www.for-less.com

Bruges for less

Compact Guide

Publisher Information

First published in Great Britain in 2000 by Metropolis International (UK) Ltd.

ISBN 1 901811 76 x

COPYRIGHT

DISCLAIMER

Assessments of attractions, hotels, museums and so forth are based on the author's impressions and therefore contain an element of subjective opinion that may not reflect the opinion of the publishers.

The contents of this publication are believed to be correct at the time of printing. However, details such as opening times will change over time. We would advise you to call ahead to confirm important information.

All organizations offering discounts in this guidebook have a contract with the publisher to give genuine discounts to holders of valid *for less* vouchers.

The publisher and/or its agents will not be responsible if any establishment breaches its contract (although it will attempt to secure compliance) or if any establishment changes ownership and the new owners refuse to honour the contract.

Care has been taken to ensure that discounts are only offered at reputable establishments, however, the publisher and/or its agents cannot accept responsibility for the quality of merchandise or service provided, nor for errors or inaccuracies in this guidebook.

The publisher will not be held responsible for any loss, damage, injury, expense or inconvenience sustained by any person, howsoever caused, as a result of information or advice contained in this guide except insofar as the law prevents the exclusion of such liability.

PUBLISHER

Metropolis International
222 Kensal Road
London W10 5BN
England

Tel:
+44-(0)20-8964-4242

Fax:
+44-(0)20-8964-4141

E-mail:
admin@for-less.com

Web site:
www.for-less.com

US Office: Tel:
+1-(212)-587-0287

Fax: +1-(212)-587-0247

ABBREVIATIONS

☎   Telephone Number
🕐   Opening times

Contents

HOW TO OBTAIN DISCOUNTS

Many of the museums and attractions in this guide offer discounts to holders of this book.

Museums and attractions which offer a discount are highlighted in pink in the text and designated by the following symbol in the margins:

To obtain your discount, simply hand in the appropriate voucher from the back of this book when you purchase your ticket.

Introduction to Bruges

Bruges is one of the gems of northern Europe. Sturdy building techniques and good fortune (it was virtually untouched in both World Wars) have ensured that its medieval skyline has survived the centuries intact. Today the city offers a cultural and architectural feast for the thousands of visitors who flock here each year.

While all European cities can lay claim to at least a smattering of historic monuments amidst their 20th-century developments, in Bruges the feeling of trespassing on a city lost in time pervades every street corner. That is not to say there are no state-of-the-art, ultra-modern shops and galleries, but their impact is modified by the timeless old buildings in which they are housed.

The profusion of **canals** – with their impressive palaces, gabled mansions and pretty bridges – creates a quaint and picturesque backdrop conducive to idle wandering. The moat and ramparts that were built at the end of the 13th century to keep Bruges' enemies out now keep the tourists in. Tourism has long replaced trade as the city's overriding business, and the inhabitants handle the sometimes overwhelming annual influx with exemplary charm.

Did You Know...?

Bruges is the most popular tourist destination in Belgium.

Wollestraat, with the Belfort in the background

Markt

One of the undisputed architectural highlights of this delightful town is the **Belfort** (Belfry). This 91m (300-ft) tower on the edge of the main square, or **Markt**, gives spectacular views of the town and an invaluable sense of orientation to first-time visitors. This appreciation of the geography of the city usually disappears, however, when visitors are once more faced with the confusion of winding streets at ground level.

As well as being a landmark on Bruges's appealing skyline, the Belfort also contributes to the atmosphere of the town with the thrice-weekly performances on its 47-bell carillon that can be heard across the rooftops.

The 17th-century gabled buildings around the **Markt** present an elegant facade on the town centre. Some of the buildings now hold modern shops and offices, but others have been put to much better use as café-bars. Here visitors and locals alike sit and watch the world go by over a cappuccino or a bowl of steaming mussels.

The city's medieval frontages are also the portals to museums rich in history, religious relics and Flemish art. Splendors also await in Bruges's ancient churches. The town boasts a priceless Michelangelo *Madonna and Child* in the **Onze Lieve Vrouwekerk**, as well as countless other works of art.

Reflections

"Somewhere within the dingy casing lay the ancient city like a notorious jewel, too stared at, talked of, trafficked over"
– Graham Greene

A picturesque canal scene

Bruges has far more good restaurants and bars than other cities of its size. The oldest establishments date back hundreds of years. They were opened to feed and entertain the merchants who founded the city and established it as a successful trading centre.

Bruges' culinary prowess is not confined to luscious handmade **chocolates**. Many cuisines are offered, but the best is perhaps the excellent, fresh seafood. Vegetarians may have a hard time, especially as most Flemish food is based on meat or fish, but there are alternatives worth seeking out.

Reflections

"...in Bruges, assailed on every side by the picturesque, you look curiously for the unpicturesque, and don't find it easily" – Arnold Bennett

As for **beer**, there are more than 300 to choose from, each served in a differently shaped bottle denoting its peculiar characteristics. They range from light fruit beers flavoured with raspberry or cherry, to dark, fearsomely strong concoctions with the consistency of treacle. That such a small country brews so many varieties never fails to surprise. Neither does the fact that so many – notably the strong ones – originate from monasteries.

Bruges is a key tourist destination, whatever the season. Spring and summer are the most popular times to visit – especially in the school holidays – but there are obvious advantages to making a winter trip.

The main one is the reduced number of tourists. The second is that the city lends itself well to wintry pleasures. Off-season visitors stand little risk of getting snow-bound, and there are often beautifully clear skies. Be aware, however, that visitors will need to wrap up against the bitter Arctic wind that whips relentlessly through the streets.

The same streets are riddled with cosy cafe-bars. It is almost worth submitting to the freezing outdoors in order to be able to rush inside and feel the life come back to your cheeks over a mug of hot chocolate or strong coffee.

At any time of year, early morning is arguably the best time to get out and about. There is something satisfying and memorable about observing the city come to life, not least for the Bruges "bicycle rush-hour", when a steady stream of cyclists rattles over the cobblestones on their way to work. They cycle quickly but courteously, their briefcases and lunch-boxes strapped to the racks behind their saddles.

Bruges's size is a real bonus. Visitors can take a leisurely walk around its **perimeter canal** in a day, and still have enough time to drop in at a windmill or enjoy a fortifying beer or two en route. For those venturing further afield, the flatness of the surrounding coastal plain makes cycling easy and fun, even for those unaccustomed to the saddle.

IF YOU DO ONE THING . . .

1. If you visit one museum . . .
the **Groeningemuseum** (page 19)

2. If you visit one church . . . the
Basilica of the Holy Blood (page 15)

3. If you photograph one bridge . . .
St. John Nepomuk Bridge (page 19)

4. If you go to one park . . .
Minnewater (page 30)

5. If you go to one bar . . .
the **Beertje** (page 55)

6. If you dine in one restaurant . . .
Den Dyver (page 50)

7. If you go to one art gallery . . .
the **Brangwynmuseum** (page 21)

8. If you go on one shopping trip . . .
the **Dijver flea market** (page 13)

9. If you go to one café . . .   the
Craenenburg (page 13)

10. If you go on one excursion . . .
Damme (page 41)

History of Bruges

Bruges began life as a 9th-century fortress built by the fierce tyrant **Baldwin I**, whose reputation earned him the daunting nickname "**Iron Arm**". As the first **count of Flanders** he was fabulously wealthy and wielded considerable power. He built the castle to repel **Viking** attacks from the North Sea.

The settlement that grew up around the castle became a successful commercial centre over the next few hundred years. By the 14th century it was regarded as a leading centre for the cloth trade and the canals were built to facilitate further the sale of goods. Its proximity to the sea meant quality wool from England could be shipped easily and cheaply across the English Channel and up the river Zwin to Bruges.

Foreign nobility travelled from far and wide to buy clothes, tapestries and lace from the numerous merchants trading in Bruges. Cloth was traded for all manner of overseas products that arrived at the docks, from exotic foodstuffs to fur coats, furniture to jewels. So powerful were the commercial traders that the town ended up heading the **Hanseatic League**, the most important trading association in medieval Europe.

Financiers too saw how well Bruges was doing and set up banks. The first stock exchange in Europe opened in the area where most traders lived and worked, now located among the crooked streets north of the central **Markt**.

The continued growth of Bruges was stifled by the on-going wrangling over ownership of the city and its surrounding region. The Bruges gentry supported Flanders as a duchy of **France** while the counts of **Flanders** and the Flemish peasants and merchants coveted indepenedence.

Trouble flared in May 1302 when the French king, **Philip the Fair**, sent troops in to restore order after the Flemish merchants refused to pay a new tax. A band of enraged merchants massacred the sleeping army. This became known as the

Reflections

"I thought that I alone was Queen; but here in this place I have six hundred rivals" — Joanna of Navarre, wife of Philip the Fair, compares herself to the splendour of Bruges.

Bruges Matins and was to spark other revolts across Flanders.

The **French** gained control in 1384 when Flanders passed to the Duke of Burgundy through marriage. Despite the accompanying upturn in Bruges' economic fortune, animosity between French and Flemish speakers continued. An element of discord still exists throughout the Flemish-speaking part of Belgium.

By the end of the 15th century, a combination of economics and geography determined Bruges' decline once more. The international cloth market slumped and the **River Zwin** silted up, severing the city's crucial link with the North Sea.

While **Antwerp** became a dominant port, Bruges slept, its medieval merchants' houses growing moss and its canals drying out. It awoke in the 19th century to find wealthy tourists marvelling at its wonderful architecture. The seeds of its 20th-century prosperity were sown.

While the Luftwaffe devestated **Rotterdam** in the Second World War, Bruges escaped largely unscathed by both World Wars. Today it is the capital of the West Flanders province. Its nearby university is a well regarded centre for European learning and its industrial periphery is known for engineering, ship-repairing, electrical goods and glass-making. More importantly, it is one of northern Europe's most visited and best loved tourist destinations.

Did You Know...?

Bruges became such an important trading centre in the 12th and 13th centuries that international banks made the city their headquarters, and the first stock exchange in Europe was held there.

De boerenadvocaat (Peasant Lawyer) *by Pieter Breughel de Younger, in the Groeningemuseum*

Central Bruges

Markt

A visitor to Bruges would do well to start exploring in the central **Markt**, right in the middle of the city. As you walk there from your hotel look out for some of the charming, narrow canals that run between the streets and buildings.

If you have not had breakfast, or feel in need of more caffeine, the northern end of the Markt is lined with cafés, housed in former merchants' guildhouses with their characteristic stepped gables, some painted bright red.

Markt

It is a good way to start the day and peruse the elegant, cobbled square in front of you. In winter they have log fires inside and umbrella burners going strong outside. Colourful flags representing the local municipalities are usually flying.

The most striking feature is the 90m (300ft) **Belfort** (Belfry, page 11) at the southern end. Most of it dates from the 13th century, as does the **Hallen** (page 12), which sits at its base.

On the eastern side of the Markt stand the imposing offices of the **Provinciaal Hof** (Provincial Government Palace, page 12), and the General Post Office, and in the middle of the square are the statues of Flemish heroes Pieter de Coninck and Jan Breydel, who spearheaded the bloody Bruges Matins revolt against a French army in 1302. In medieval times the Markt was the site for public executions, and a gallows stood here for many years.

Built predominantly in the 13th century, the **Belfort** (Belfry) is a tall and impressive symbol of great pride for the city. Although it is not obvious to the naked eye, this octagonal tower actually leans by a foot or more.

Between the base of the Belfort, where the old cloth market stood, and the bells and pigeons at the top, lie 366 steps which are worth climbing if you don't mind aching calves and close encounters with schoolchildren. The steps pass the complicated workings of a giant clock and music box which pulls the bell ropes automatically. It gets crowded at the top at lunchtime as people try to get up there for the deafening midday chimes.

The view is both breathtaking and terrifying, depending on your love or hatred of heights. It is also a good place to get your bearings and admire the red terracotta roofs. Bruges from this angle looks more like a town in southern France or Spain than on the chilly north European plain.

The design is not so surprising when you learn that Spaniards flocked here from the late 15th century to escape the Inquisition.

At night the Belfort glows with orange light and looks like a giant candle warming the centre of the city. Three times a week during the summer the whole town is treated to a full-scale concert from the magnificent 18th-century carillon, which features no fewer than 47 bells.

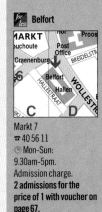

Belfort

Markt 7
☎ 40 56 11
🕐 Mon–Sun:
9.30am–5pm.
Admission charge.
2 admissions for the price of 1 with voucher on page 67.

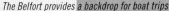

The Belfort provides a backdrop for boat trips

The Belfort lit up at night

Back in medieval times the **Hallen** (Covered Market) must have been a frantic place as merchants set up their stalls on the cobblestones and traded furiously, their customers haggling with them over the prices of cloth and lace.

This was the centre of commercial activity for many years in Bruges and it laid the economic bedrock on which the city's success was built.

Some of the carving on the wooden galleries you see today is much more modern but it is not hard to picture the scene 600 years ago as money and goods changed hands amid much excitement.

The tall neo-Gothic **Provinciaal Hof** (Provincial Government Palace) houses the West Flanders provincial government and takes up much of the eastern side of the Markt.

Hallen

Markt 7

It dates from the beginning of the 20th century, but in spite of this fits well with the rest of the square's much older buildings. Its roof is steep and high and punctuated with pinnacled turrets, reminiscent of a Luxembourg castle or French chateau.

The building is located on the site of a former landing dock where barges would tie up after their trip up the river from the North Sea to unload their cargoes. It was the perfect mooring point for merchants as the Hallen open-air market was only

100 yards away at the base of the Belfort.

The Provinciaal Hof is a working office and official government chamber and is not open to the public.

The **Craenenburg** café, on the corner of the Markt and St. Amandsstraat, is so popular it can be difficult to get a seat. It is written about more than the other cafés because on this site once stood a house in which the heir to the Hapsburg throne, Archduke Maximilian, was imprisoned by the Bruges authorities in the late 15th century. The future Emperor always held a grudge against Bruges as a result and favoured Antwerp for trade, hastening Bruges's economic decline.

The Craenenburg is a good place to view the illuminated Belfort over a late evening glass of Calvados, the cider brandy from Normandy, which comes to your table in a warmed glass.

Near the Craenenburg is the 15th-century, brick-built **Huis Bouchoute** (Bouchoute House), which has the oldest frontage of any house in the square. It is not open to the public.

A short walk from the Markt down Breidelstraat is the **Burg**, which was the city's original main square and is more elegant even than the Markt. The grey stone buildings have been cleaned in recent years and their facades shine in the sunlight.

On the western side of the Burg near the entrance from Breidelstraat stands the **Proosdij** (Provost's House, page 14), former home to the church elders.

Along the southern edge of the square is the **Stadhuis** (page 14), said to be the oldest town hall in Belgium and certainly one of the most handsome. It is another good example of bold Gothic architecture, some of it original, some of it modern reproduction.

In the corner to the west of the Stadhuis is the **Basiliek van het Heilig Bloed** (Basilica of the Holy Blood, page 15), arguably Bruges's chief tourist attraction.

Along the eastern flank of the Burg lies

Provinciaal Hof

Markt 3
🕐 Not open to the public.

Craenenburg café

Markt 16
☎ 33 34 02
🕐 Mon-Fri, Sun: 7.30am-11pm. Sat: 7.30am-1am.

Huis Bouchoute

Markt
🕐 Not open to the public.

Burg

the **Gerechtshof**, otherwise known as the Paleis van het Brugse Vrije (page 16), which until just a few years ago was the law courts but now houses various administrative offices for the city authorities. Included among them is the **Tourist Information Centre**, which is well worth a quick visit early on in your stay to pick up brochures and city maps and find out what's on that week.

The grey stone **Proosdij** (Provost's House) dates from the 1660s and used to be home for the elders of the church of St. Donatian, which stood at the north eastern end of the Burg (now inhabited by a Holiday Inn which shows off some foundation stones).

The church was destroyed just over 100 years later and today it is remembered by a miniature stone model near the trees that stand in the centre of the square.

In front of the Proosdij stands a statue of Justice with her sword and scales, and nearby is a bronze sculpture entitled *The Lovers*. It represents the many couples who have been married in the Stadhuis (below), often in haste, as depicted by the blindfolds over the lovers' eyes.

The **Stadhuis** (Town Hall) was built between 1376 and 1420 and has undergone several facelifts at the hands of stonemasons over the years. Statues of

Tourist Information Centre

Burg 11
☎ 44 86 86
⏰ Apr-Sep: Mon-Fri: 9.30am-6.30pm. Sat-Sun: 10am-12noon, 2pm-6.30pm. Oct-Mar: Mon-Fri: 9.30am-5pm. Sat: 9.30am-1.15pm, 2pm-5.30pm. Sun: closed.

The Stadhuis

successive counts and countesses of Flanders were sculpted and put in place in a row along the outside wall in medieval times but fell victim to French hatred and were smashed. The ones you see today are modern replicas.

The two main doors are framed by high stone arches and the battlements at the top of the facade are broken up by three elegant, slender turrets topped with spires. The Stadhuis is used frequently for receptions and weddings.

Inside, a stairway leads visitors up to the magnificent **Gotische Zaal Stadhuis** (Gothic Chamber). This room, still the working council chamber, is lavishly decorated with red and gold and has a remarkable vaulted ceiling with late-medieval carving. The intricate murals were added during restoration in the 19th century and show scenes from the Bible and important milestones in the history of Bruges, while the adjoining chamber features a display of documents and art charting the same.

The small **Basiliek van het Heilig Bloed** is situated in the south-western corner of the Burg. It is an international site of pilgrimage for the faithful and a major tourist attraction for all.

To find the entrance look for an elegant facade of intricately carved stone arches, with painted shields built into them, and fine gilded statues of knights in battledress holding their swords to attention. Above the entrance rise two towers of Islamic design.

In the **Heilig Bloed Kapel** (Chapel of the Holy Blood), reached by a sweeping staircase, is a phial made of crystal which is believed to have contained a few drops of blood from Christ's wounds, collected by Joseph of Arimathea at the Crucifixion.

It was brought to Bruges in the middle of the 12th century by a knight and Count of Flanders, Derick (or Dietrich) of Alsace, who had been given it in Jerusalem as a gift for his bravery in the Crusades.

After drying out for some years, the solidified film of blood was reported to

Proosdij

Burg 3
🕐 Not open to the public.

Gotische Zaal Stadhuis

Burg 12
🕐 Mon-Sun:
9.30am-5pm.
Admission charge.
2 admissions for the price of 1 with voucher on page 67.

Basiliek van het Heilig Bloed

Burg 13
☎ 33 67 92
🕐 Apr-Sep: Mon-Sun:
9.30am-12noon, 2pm-6pm. Oct-Mar: Mon-Tue,
Thu-Sun: 10am-12noon,
2pm-4pm.
Wed: 10am-12noon.
Admission charge.

have begun liquifying on Friday evenings until 1325. A number of leading clerics from the 13th and early 14th century swore to the event.

Every Friday, to this day, a line of visitors waits at the chapel as the relic is brought out and displayed from 8.30am to 11.45am and then from 3pm to 4pm for veneration They file past and can receive a blessing from the priest. It is a silent, sombre occasion and worth the wait.

If you are in Bruges on Ascension Day, you will be able to watch the colourful **Heilig Bloedprocessie** (Procession of the Holy Blood). The phial is placed in a gold and silver reliquary and carried through the streets with great pomp and ceremony.

Renaissanceszaal Brugse Vrije

Burg 11
☎ 44 82 60
⏰ Mon-Sun: 9.30am-
12.30pm, 1.30pm-5pm.
Admission charge.
2 admissions for the price of 1 with voucher on page 67.

It is the most impressive public event in this part of northern Europe. At other times of the year the reliquary is displayed behind protective glass in the **Museum of the Holy Blood**, just next to the chapel, which also contains other religious artefacts and paintings. (☎ 44 87 11. ⏰ *Apr-Sep: 9.30am-12pm & 2pm-6pm. Oct-Mar: 10am-12pm & 2pm-4pm. Closed on Wednesday afternoons. Admission charge).*

Downstairs from the Heilig Bloed Kapel is **St. Basil's Chapel**, so named because his bones, also brought back from the Crusades, were said to have lain there. It is worth a quick look around to get an idea of the more simple, stark style of medieval church design.

The **Oude Griffie** (Old Recorder's House) stands next to the Stadhuis. It dates back to the middle of the 16th century and used to house the official city records. For the last hundred years or more it has been used as an anteroom to the law courts next door. The public are not allowed into the Oude Griffie. *(Burg 11a.)*

The **Gerechtshof**, or **Paleis van het Brugse Vrije** (Palace of the Freeman of Bruges) was built in 1520 and extensively reconstructed two hundred years later. The original building was the residence of the Counts of Flanders, and after rebuilding it became home to the Courts of Justice until the 1980s.

The **Renaissanceszaal Brugse Vrije** (Renaissance Hall of the Freeman of Bruges) can be visited. The sole exhibit is a giant Renaissance chimneypiece made from oak and black marble – a homage to the ruler of the day, the Emperor Charles V. The ornately carved exhibit has survived from the early part of the 16th century.

It was designed by the artist Lancelot Blondeel and finished in 1531. It is an unashamed boast on behalf of the Hapsburgs, showing carvings of Charles himself and both sets of grandparents from the Austrian and Spanish sides all bursting with pride. Charles is featured wearing an enormous codpiece, as if to make absolutely clear the prowess and importance of the Hapsburg lineage.

Blinde Ezelstraat

Although this is all there is in the museum it's worth a trip as it must rank as one of the most important and visually stunning pieces of art in the city. The very fact that it has survived in such good condition since it was made more than 450 years ago is reason enough to visit.

Bruges is a city for walking and one of the easiest and most picturesque starts is the Burg at the entrance to the alleyway between the Oude Griffie and the Stadhuis. It is marked by a Renaissance arch and leads down to **Blinde Ezelstraat** (Blind Donkey Street).

You will cross the main canal on one of

Heilig Bloedprocessie

Bruges's famous stone bridges (that is how the city got its name) and come to a covered colonnade, the **Vismarkt** (Fish Market), which dates from the 1820s. On market days, vast fish are sliced up and sold from the stone slabs.

You can follow the canal along streets on either side. If you opt for Groenerei you will walk past the **Pelicaanhuis** (Pelican House),

Huidenvettersplein

recognizable by the pelican sign over the door. This was probably an almshouse at some time, a place to house the infirm or poor.

Vismarkt

Tue-Sat: 6am-1pm.
Sun-Mon: closed.

If you go behind the Vismarkt instead you will find the **Huidenvettersplein** (Tanners' Square) and its 17th-century, turreted **Huidenvettershuis** (Tanners' Guildhall) where members of the trade body would meet.

If you have had enough of walking and feel like taking one of the many canal rides through Bruges, then just near the tanners' quarter is the **Rozenhoedkaai** (Rosary Quay) where you can step aboard a boat.

Huidenvettershuis

Huidenvettersplein
Not open to the public.

The canal tours are good. Sometimes the boats look as if they are about to collide in a narrow stretch of canal but they always manage to avoid each other. The commentary from the guides is not too detailed – just enough to give you a flavour of what life was like in medieval times when Bruges was in its economic prime.

Bruges has earned a reputation for having smelly canals in the summer but they are no worse than Venice or any other watery city. In fact they are charming and worth exploring at your leisure.

South Bruges

Next to the Rozenhoedkaai canal boat landing is a bridge, the **Sint Jan Nepomucenusbrug** (St. John Nepomuk Bridge) which was put up at the start of the 19th century and supports a statue of this patron saint of bridges.

St. John Nepomuk earned his title rather painfully. He was hurled from a bridge into a river (not in Bruges but somewhere in Bohemia, it is believed) for refusing to divulge to King Wenceslas IV of Bohemia the confessions the queen had made to him in church.

From the Sint Jan Nepomucenusbrug you can walk along the banks of the river **Dijver**, which runs through the centre of Bruges. At the weekend there is a fascinating flea market along here, selling everything from giant copper cooking pans to chimney pots and cast-iron shoe-scrapers that need two people to lift them.

The houses along the river front are among the most picturesque and well preserved in Bruges. Further on the river passes a collection of museums, containing some of the finest works and relics in northern Europe.

The **Groeningemuseum** houses a rich and

Sint Jan Nepomucenusbrug

The Dijver

fascinating collection of six centuries of Flemish, Dutch and Belgian painting. The museum's many highlights include the world-famous collection of early Flemish paintings, known also as the Flemish Primitives, by a wide range of Renaissance masters. They include disturbing works from Hieronymus Bosch such as the *Last Judgement*, which portrays his terrifying vision of hell's flames reaching out to grab the ungodly and suck them under the earth.

Groeningemuseum

Brangwynmuseum/Kantmu (Arentshuis)

Groeningemuseum

't Leerhu

Dijver 12
☎ 44 87 62
🕐 Apr-Sep: Mon-Sun: 9.30am-5pm. Oct-Mar: Wed-Mon: 9.30am-5pm. Tue: closed.
Admission charge.
2 admissions for the price of 1 with voucher on page 67.

A mainstay of the Primitives is Jan van Eyck. Of note is his *Madonna with Canon George van der Paele* (1436), which shows the Madonna holding Christ with St. George and St. Donatian and the Canon kneeling to one side of her. They are all surrounded by the opulence that van Eyck would have seen in Bruges at the time he painted it, when the city was thriving on the cloth trade. Also, look out for the portrait of the painter's wife, Margareta van Eyck.

The same luxurious trappings can be seen in the paintings by Rogier van der Weyden, also on display here.

Wonderful as the museum is, a lot of the more gruesome, violent works take courage to view. In the Bruges painter Gerard David's *The Judgement of Cambyses* (1498), the corrupt Persian judge Sisamnes is being flayed in public at the behest of Cambyses, ancient king of

Madonna with Canon George van der Paele, *van Eyck*

Persia, with many passers-by seeming not even to notice, let alone care. For a while the painting hung in the Stadhuis by way of appeasement to Archduke Maximilian. Held captive by the burghers of Bruges in 1488 for three months in a house in the Markt, he later became Holy Roman Emperor.

Stilleven met waaier, Brusselmans

There is a selection of paintings from the late 16th and early 17th centuries including ones by Pieter Bruegel the Younger, Pieter Pourbus and Jacob van Oost the Elder who was prolific during the baroque period in Bruges.

There are works dating from the 18th- and 19th-century neo-classical and Realist periods, and a collection of milestones of Belgian Symbolism and Modernism.

Some of the masterpieces by Flemish Expressionists are newly on display and worth a look, as are some of those from the city's collection of post-war modern art which includes works by James Ensor and Magritte.

The **Arenthuis** building on Dijver is home to both the **Brangwynmuseum** (below) and the **Kant Museum** (page 22). If you are walking there after seeing the wonders of the Groeningemuseum then you will pass through a garden and over a humpback bridge which is worth a photo. Of course, every other tourist to Bruges has taken the same one but it is picturesque with its backdrop of ancient brick houses.

One entrance fee is charged for visiting both museums housed in the Arenthuis. On the first floor is the **Brangwynmuseum**, named after the painter Sir Frank

for less **Brangwynmuseum and Kant Museum**

Arenthuis, Dijver 16
☎ 44 87 63
⏲ Apr-Sep: Mon-Sun: 9.30am-5pm. Oct-Mar: Wed-Mon: 9.30am-5pm. Tue: closed.
Admission charge.
2 admissions for the price of 1 with voucher on page 67.

A display of lace in the Kant Museum

Brangwyn. Although of Welsh origin, Brangwyn was born in Bruges in 1867 and lived there for the first few years of his life. He always held a strong affinity for his birthplace and donated a collection of his work to the city before his death in 1956.

Despite Brangwyn's bold use of colour, many of his works are melancholy. The collection comprises paintings, drawings and prints as well as furniture and carpets.

He drew scenes of the dockside barges, silent after the working day, and through the trees and from across the Minnewater, he observed and drew the Beguines (page 29).

Downstairs is the **Kant Museum**, a collection of lace. For many years in medieval times Bruges was the centre of Europe's lace trade. Merchants in the Hallen market by the Belfort traded with their counterparts from around the world who would bring exotic gifts from afar with which to barter.

This museum has displays of lace dating back to the 16th century as well as a selection of ceramics and horse-drawn carriages. You can still buy lace in Bruges today (see page 53). You are almost guaranteed good quality but it can be expensive.

The 15th-century former mansion which houses the **Gruuthusemuseum** (Gruuthuse Museum) on Dijver once belonged to a man who must have been the scourge of Bruges's beer makers. He was responsible for collecting taxes on *gruut*, a herbal mix which used to be added to the barley during the brewing process instead of yeast.

The building itself, much of which has been restored, is a fascinating study of medieval architecture. Note the thick cross beams and impressive chimneypieces that act as backdrops for the collection of art and artefacts on display here.

The Gruuthusemuseum gives the visitor a good idea of the extent of opulence that was enjoyed in Bruges during its commercial heyday in medieval times. Wealthy merchants and businessmen such as the owner of this house must have lived in incomparable splendour.

In every room you will find antique furniture and collections of miscellaneous items such as kitchen scales, travelling trunks, weapons, Delft chinaware, even a barrel organ. There are exquisite tapestries hanging on the walls, some dating back 400 years.

Keep an eye out for the wood and terracotta bust of Charles V carved in 1520, and the small chapel that sticks out from the second floor via a gallery. This

Gruuthusemuseum

Dijver 17
☎ 448 762
⏲ Reopens June 2000.
Apr-Sep: Mon-Sun:
9.30am-5pm. Oct-Mar:
Wed-Mon: 9.30am-5pm.
Tue: closed.
Admission charge.
2 admissions for the price of 1 with voucher on page 67.

Gruuthusemuseum

leads into the Onze Lieve Vrouwekerk (Church of Our Lady) next door and allowed the owners of the house their own private route to church.

Onze Lieve Vrouwekerk

Mariastraat
☎ 44 86 86
🕐 Apr-Sep: Mon-Fri: 10am-11.30am, 2.30pm-5pm. Sat: 10am-11.30am, 2.30pm-4pm. Sun: 2.30pm-4pm.
Oct-Mar: Mon-Fri: 10am-11.30am, 2.30pm-4.30pm. Sat: 10am-11.30am, 2.30pm-4pm. Sun: 2.30pm-4.30pm.
Admission charge.

The main spire of the magnificent **Onze Lieve Vrouwekerk** rises to 121m (400 feet) and towers above the rest of Bruges. It is one of the city's key landmarks and can be seen for miles across the flat Flanders plain. When ships still sailed up the rivers Zwin and Reie into the heart of Bruges to dock where the Provinciaal Hof (Provincial Government Palace, page 12) now stands in the Markt, they could judge the distance to their destination by watching the spire.

However, impressive as the great pinnacle is, the church (located on the Dijver) is not the most picturesque of buildings in the city. In fact it's rather bleak and grey, and it's the interior that is special.

Do not be surprised to be met just inside the south door by a woman telling you rather sharply to be quiet and holding a placard with red writing ordering silence. She is there mainly to keep unruly school groups in line. The church gets crowded in the summer months and it is best to time your visit at the beginning or end of the day and avoid weekends if possible.

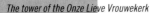

The tower of the Onze Lieve Vrouwekerk

Most people flock to the Church of Our Lady to see one thing - the _Madonna and Child_ marble sculpture by Michelangelo which dates from the first few years of the 16th century. Its great beauty and craftsmanship seem a bit lost in this rather austere church. The protective glass screen does little to enhance the

sculpture's grace but no doubt saves it from desecration.

The Madonna was brought to Bruges by a wealthy Flemish merchant and donated to the church. It was the only sculpture to leave Italy during Michelangelo's lifetime. Many artists in northern Europe at the time visited the church and took great inspiration from it.

The paintings hanging in the church include *Adoration of the Shepherds* and *The Last Supper* by Pieter Pourbus, *The Transfiguration* by Gerard David and Jan van Eyck's famous *Christ on the Cross*. The baroque pulpit is flamboyant and draped with cherubs.

If you want to get in to the choir to see the tombs of Charles the Bold and his daughter Mary of Burgundy you will have to pay a fee, which is worth it for they are intricately carved. Charles was killed at the battle of Nancy in 1477 and Mary after a horse-riding accident in 1482 when she was only 25. You can look through small windows into the crypt where Mary's coffin lies. Look out also for the gallery that links the church with the Gruuthuse next door.

The **Archeologisch Museum** is nearby. It contains a collection of artefacts discovered during excavations in the city, which provide an insight into Bruges's past. Pieces on display include glass and pottery items, leather and metalwork, and murals. They date from the Stone Age to the Middle Ages.

The **Sint Salvatorskathedraal** (St. Saviour's Cathedral) was never built to be a cathedral which explains why it lacks some of the pomp and grandeur of other churches in the city. But when the French destroyed the cathedral of St. Donatian which stood in the Burg in 1799, St. Saviour's was chosen as its successor.

It was officially named as Bruges's new cathedral in 1834 and five years later disaster struck when fired raged through the building and destroyed the roof and tower. Parts of the building date back to the early 15th century, notably the choir stalls, although these cannot be visited by the public. The rest of the architecture,

Archeologisch Museum

Mariastraat 36a
☎ 44 87 30
🕐 Tue, Thu, Sat and Sun: 9.30am-12.30pm, 1.30pm-5pm.
Admission charge.
2 admissions for the price of 1 with voucher on page 69.

Sint Salvatorskathedraal

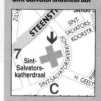

Steenstraat
☎ 34 20 22
🕐 Cathedral and museum: Summer: Mon-Sat: 10am-11.30am, 2pm-5pm. Sun: 10am-11.30am, 3pm-5pm. Winter: Mon-Tue, Thu-Sat: 2pm-5pm. Wed & Sun: closed.
Admission charge.

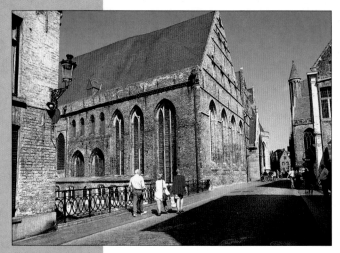

Sint Janshospitaal

Steenstraat

interior design and furniture is a mix of different styles through the ages, added bit by bit as the church has been renovated. The vast baroque organ and statue of God both date from the late 17th century.

Some remarkable tapestries hang on the walls and there is a small museum next to the north transept which houses a collection of ecclesiastical artefacts.

A good and quite short walk through some of Bruges's most picturesque alleyways is based on the area around **Steenstraat**, just north of Sint Salvatorskathedraal. As long as you have the map handy you won't get lost, although part of the fun of Bruges is following your nose and finding out where you end up.

Hof Van Watervliet

Oude Burg 27
🕐 Not open to the public.

The street itself is charming. It is a typically elegant jumble of brightly painted houses with stepped gables.

If you carry on down the street it will lead you back to the Markt but instead head back past Simon Stevinplein and carry on to **Oude Burg**, where the **Hof Van Watervliet** stands, a 16th-century house which can boast some prestigious guests over the centuries. Erasmus, the humanist, stayed here, as did Charles II of England who came here in exile.

Mariastraat runs from the Oude Burg past the Onze Lieve Vrouwekerk to some other places of interest further south. It is attractive in itself, with pretty almshouses. Watch for a turning into the narrowest street in Bruges, **Stoofstraat** (page 28), and the entrance to the **Huisbrouwerij Straffe Hendrik** (Strong Henry Brewery, page 28).

The **Sint Janshospitaal** (St. John's Hospital), just off Mariastraat, was a hospital back in medieval times and operated as one for several hundreds of years. Today it houses in its former chapel the **Memlingmuseum**, dedicated to the painter Hans Memling, who was in fact German by birth. He became a pupil of Rogier van der Weyden and spent most of his working life in Bruges. He is known today as one of the most prolific of the Flemish masters.

Probably his most famous work in this collection is the *Reliquary of St. Ursula*, thought to have been painted in the mid-15th century. The work is a painted, wooden, miniature church which depicts the story of St. Ursula and more than 10,000 virgins who were supposedly murdered in Germany while on their way to Rome, so becoming Christian martyrs. There is some speculation, however, that the number of virgins in the story might have been exaggerated somewhat as the painted wooden panels show only ten accompanying the saint to Rome.

Regardless of the actual accuracy of the story or his painting, Memling was known for his ceaseless attention to detail and this is one of the works most representative of his skill.

Among the other Memlings in the museum are the *Mystic Marriage of*

Memlingmuseum

Mariastraat 38
☎ 44 87 11
🕐 Reopens October 2000. Apr-Sep: Mon-Sun: 9.30am-5pm. Oct-Mar: Thu-Tue: 9.30am-5pm. Wed: closed.
Admission charge.
2 admissions for the price of 1 with voucher on page 69.

Kruisdraging *by Jan Provost, Memlingmuseum*

Walstraat

Brouwerij Straffe Hendrik

Walplein 26
☎ 33 26 97
⏰ Apr-Sep: Mon-Sun:
10am-5pm. Oct-Mar:
Mon-Sun: 11am-3pm.
Admission charge; guided
tours only (includes one
drink).

St. Catherine, which shows an infant Jesus placing a ring on St. Catherine's finger, the *Adoration of the Magi* and several fine portraits.

There is also a wonderful, renovated chemist's dispensary in the former hospital building dating back to the 17th century. The walls are lined with shelves holding a range of potions and salts. The drawers in the long counter are sagging with age, and in the middle of the room stand two elaborate mixing bowls.

Stoofstraat, off Mariastraat, is famous for being the narrowest street in Bruges, and just beyond it **Walstraat** leads away. This is one of Bruges's more picturesque streets, again lined with wonderful, step-gabled houses.

The **Brouwerij Straffe Hendrik** (Strong Henry Brewery) in Walplein produces a beer of the same name (Strong Henry). Visitors can take a pungent, guided tour of the brewery which lasts nearly an hour and includes a free glass of beer at the end.

The **Begijnhof** (Place of the Beguines), which is in the south of the city near the Minnewater, is the area where the Beguines came to live. They were unmarried or deserted women who wanted to live like nuns but without taking the full vows and joining a religious order. However, they were involved in many of the charitable works normally associated with nuns, such as caring for the elderly and the sick.

The Begijnhof is one of the greenest and most beautiful parts of Bruges. It is believed a vineyard once stood here. It is reached by crossing a bridge over the canal. The Beguines lived in an arc of white-washed, 17th-century almshouses which are preserved and occupied to this day.

The women you might see here today are not Beguines, however, but members of an order of Benedictine nuns who still wear the habits favoured by the Beguines. There is a church dating back to the beginning of the 17th century which has a basic wooden interior design.

One of the houses, the **Begijnhuisje**, acts as a small museum open to the public. It gives visitors a glimpse of the life of a Beguine, highlighting the sparseness of possessions and the lack of luxury they opted for when choosing this style of life. This part of Bruges is another example of how well preserved the city is – little has changed here since medieval times.

The lack of cars in the city is a blessing and makes walking through its streets much more enjoyable. If you want to get away from shops and museums altogether, then head for some of Bruges's beautiful open spaces.

South of Walplein, Wijngaardplein and the Begijnhof lies the popular park of **Minnewater** (The Lake of Love) with

Begijnhuisje

Wijngaardplein
☎ 33 00 11
🕐 Church and Begijnhof:
Mon-Sun: 6am-12noon,
2.30pm-6pm.
Admission free.
🕐 Begijnhuisje: Dec-Feb:
Wed, Thu, Sat, Sun:
2.45pm-4.15pm. Fri:
1.45pm-6pm. Mar, Oct,
Nov: 10.30am-12noon,
1.45pm-5pm. Apr-Sep:
Mon-Sat: 10am-12noon,
1.45pm-5.30pm (not Fri
morning). Sun: 10am-
12noon, 1.45pm-6pm.
Admission charge.
**2 admissions for the price
of 1 with voucher on page
69.**

Entrance to the Begijnhof

The Begijnhof

its resident swans. Before the rivers from the North Sea silted up and stifled Bruges's trade, this expanse of water served as part of the city's harbour. There are the remains of some 14th-century fortifications to see as well as good views back across the Bruges skyline. Minnewater is where the citizens of Bruges come to relax on sunny weekend afternoons.

South-east of the Burg, near the church of St. Magdalena, lies the **Koningin Astridpark** with pleasant landscaped walkways and gardens, and a children's playground.

Minnewater

The **'t Zand**, not far from the Sint Salvatorskathedraal, is where a large public market is held each Saturday morning. On days when the place is clear of stalls look out for the group of modern statues standing in the middle of the square. They were sculpted by local artists and put up in 1985. The four distinct groups represent different regions and characteristics of Flanders.

If it is thrills you are looking for try the **Boudewijnpark**, a large, permanent funfair a little way south of Bruges. There is a variety of rides, crazy golf and a dolphinarium. *(A. Debaeckestraat 13, ☎ 38 38 38. ⏲ May-Aug, Easter, weekends in Sep: 11am-6pm. Admission charge.)*

Koningin Astridpark

Most of the defensive **Vesten en Poorten** (walls and gates) which form a ring around the city were put up at the end of the 13th century, when Bruges was already a wealthy, thriving trade centre and in need of protection. There was a moat too, for extra security, which drained water from nearby rivers.

The complex canal system was also put in place at this time, its channels winding through the city centre to aid the transport of goods from ships that had docked in the outer harbour (now the Minnewater, page 29).

Some sections of the walls still remain and are covered by earth banks, but it is the seven former fortified gates that have survived so well and look so impressive.

Visitors can take a picturesque and fascinating walk by making their way to the nearest point on the perimeter canal, heading either clockwise or anti-clockwise and following the water right around the city centre. They will be able to trace the path of the former ramparts and stop off at the various gates along the way.

Gentpoort is one of the most visually stunning. It comprises a pair of bulky, impenetrable round towers with a narrow gateway between them. It dates from the 14th century and guarded the route leading out of the city to the south-east and Ghent. The gate must have looked a daunting prospect for any would-be invader.

Smedenpoort (The Blacksmith's Gate) protected the city from attack from the west. It was the only gate that allowed two-way traffic.

't Zand

🕐 Market: Sat: 7am-1pm.

Gentpoort

Gunpowder Tower overlooking Minnewater

North Bruges

Sint Jacobskerk (St. Jacob's Church) dates back to the 13th century and is a good deal brighter and more cheerful inside than many of Bruges's other places of worship. You will find it in Sint-Jakobsstraat, west of Jan van Eyckplein. The church has undergone much restoration over the centuries, made possible primarily by monetary gifts from the Dukes of Burgundy. It is decorated with a collection of paintings from the 16th to the 18th centuries.

Sint Jacobskerk

St. Jakobstraat

Jan van Eyckplein is one of the main squares in the district north of the Markt. There used to be a large harbour here where boats that had navigated up river from the North Sea would dock and unload. In medieval times it must have been a blur of activity as exotic foodstuffs, elaborately carved furniture and luxurious furs were carried ashore.

Now the streets and canals are quiet and make an ideal environment for a peaceful stroll. You will find fewer tour groups in this part of the city as it is quite a way off the main museum and sight-seeing trail.

The canal that begins at the square and heads north-east winds out of the centre of the city and across the outer ring of water near the ring road. From there it widens to become a major waterway that connects Bruges to **Sluis**, a town just over the border in Holland. En route it passes

A canal boat tour

Speigelrei

the pretty medieval town of **Damme** (page 41), 7km (4 miles) north-east of Bruges.

The square is a good place to begin a cycle ride or walk to Damme, following the **Speigelrei** and **Lange Rei** roads north until you reach the **Noorweegsekaai**. The path lies next to the canal which is shaded by poplar trees, and the route is dead flat all the way. In the 14th century, Spiegelrei was a street full of overseas trade missions, all fiercely marketing their countries' products.

The Noorweegsekaai is also the mooring point for a paddle steamer that runs between there and Damme during the summer months. It goes so slowly you will hardly know it is moving and may well get overtaken by walkers on the bank. It offers the most leisurely outing in Bruges.

It is widely believed that Europe's first stock exchange was here in Bruges, in a 15th-century house on Grauwwerkerstraat, west of Jan van Eyckplein. The **Huis ter Beurze** was owned by a wealthy merchant by the name of Van Der Beurze, which explains why in many European countries today a stock exchange is known as a *bourse*.

Several other merchants traded in the house and nearby. With Bruges's great wealth in the medieval period it seems fitting that such an institution was set up here. Merchants came from all over

Huis ter Beurze

Vlamingstraat 35
🕐 Not open to the public.

Statue of Jan van Eyck

Europe and beyond, as the wonderful cloth the city produced was in great demand.

Opposite the Huis ter Beurze stands the **Natiehuis van Genua** (Genoese Trading House), where the Genoese merchants were based. It too dates from the 15th century.

Memories of Bruges's golden age abound here. On the north side of Jan van Eyckplein stands the 15th century **Oud Tolhuis** (Old Tollhouse). On its facade is emblazoned the coat of arms of the Dukes of Luxembourg who gathered tolls from traders here. *(Jan van Eyckplein 2.)*

Above the terracotta rooftops can be seen the tower of the **Poortersloge**, a meeting place for the most wealthy and influential of the Bruges merchants.

There are two churches worth seeing in the district. Leave the square by Spinolarei street, turn right into Koningstraat and then left into St. Maartensplein where stands **St. Walburgakerk** (Church of St. Walburga). It is a striking baroque building dating from the middle of the 17th century and designed by Pieter Huyssens, a Bruges Jesuit.

Inside, the first thing to catch the eye is the remarkable wooden pulpit which leans into the centre of the church at such a precarious angle that it looks as if it is defying gravity.

On the other side of the canal is **St. Annakerk** (Church of St. Anne) in the street of the same name. This church is just a few years older than St. Walburgakerk and also baroque, with intricate wooden carvings inside. It stands

St. Walburgakerk

St. Maartensplein

St. Annakerk

St. Annaplein

on the site of an even earlier church.

Based on the design of the Church of the Holy Sepulchre in Jerusalem, the **Jeruzalemkerk**, situated on Peperstraat, was built in 1427-8 by the Adornes, a family of Genoese merchants. Before that, a chapel built by the same family had stood here since the 13th century.

The Adornes had been inspired by a pilgrimage to Jerusalem and wanted to create a replica of the Holy Sepulchre in homage. The Jeruzalemkerk's many-sided tower is distinctive and sets it apart from the other churches in the city.

Inside, one of the highlights is the stained glass which dates from the 15th and 16th centuries. Anselm Adornes and his wife are buried in the church, which is still owned by their descendants.

Some visitors find the brick-built church a little eerie which is understandable. The natural lighting is poor, there are several dark, forbidding corners, and the stone altarpiece is decorated with skulls, bones and ladders.

The church does, however, have some more cheering qualities, including a stone staircase leading up from the lower level to a small door to the left of the altar, above which is a charming rose window of clear glass with a yellow shield in its centre.

The Adornes family also donated money to build some almshouses which still stand today, although now they are occupied by the **Kantcentrum** (Lace Centre). Visitors keen to find out how the finest lace in the world is made and how in medieval times it put Bruges on the map as a leading city in the textile industry would enjoy a visit here.

On display are fine examples of the most delicate cuffs and collars, worn as adornments to clothes, as well as table decorations and handkerchiefs. There is a group of lacemakers who give demonstrations of their craft and can answer questions as they work feverishly at their cushions.

Also of interest in this part of the city is the **Museum voor Volkskunde** (Folklore Museum). It is situated at the north end

Jeruzalemkerk

Peperstraat 3a
☎ 33 00 72
🕐 Mon-Fri: 10am-12noon, 2pm-6pm. Sat: 10am-12noon, 2pm-5pm. Sun: closed.
Admission charge.

Kantcentrum

Peperstraat 3a
☎ 33 00 72
🕐 Mon-Fri: 10am-12noon, 2pm-6pm. Sat: 10am-12noon, 2pm-5pm. Sun: closed.
Admission charge.

Museum voor Volkskunde

Rolweg 40
☎ 44 87 11
🕐 Apr-Sep: Mon-Sun: 9.30am-5pm. Oct-Mar: Wed-Mon: 9.30am-5pm. Tue: closed.
Admission charge.
2 admissions for the price of 1 with voucher on page 69.

Museum voor Volkskunde

Guido Gezellemuseum

Rolweg 64

☎ 44 87 66

🕒 Apr-Sep: Mon-Sun: 9.30am-12.30pm, 1.30pm-5pm. Oct-Mar: Wed-Mon: 9.30am-12.30pm, 1.30pm-5pm. Admission charge.
2 admissions for the price of 1 with voucher on page 69.

of Balstraat, on Rolweg at the sign of De Zwarte Kat (Black Cat), and it too occupies a line of almshouses.

The museum offers a flashback to the life of everyday Bruges folk over the centuries. There is a faithful recreation of a chemist's shop with high ceiling and shelves laden with elegantly labelled bottles and stone jars, an oak-beamed coffee shop with large weighing scales, and a traditional bar (The Black Cat).

Almost every trade is represented. There are workshops for a milliner, cobbler and cooper. There is a schoolroom with globe and abacus, and a family kitchen.

The **Guido Gezellemuseum**, situated near the Museum voor Volkskunde on Rolweg, is dedicated to one of Flanders most famous poets. Guido Gezelle (1830-99) was born and grew up in Bruges where he became a priest in 1854. This museum, in his former residence, contains a collection of books and souvenirs documenting his life.

For a citizen of Bruges, being a member of one of the prestigious Archery Guilds was a social must. Both main guildhalls have small museums that are open to the public. The headquarters of the **Sint-Sebastiaansgilde** (Guild of Longbow Archers) are in a building in Carmerstraat where the guild has met for many years.

Today it is a shrine to the sport. The walls of the grand main room are lined with portraits of former members and beneath them a collection of light wooden canons and ceremonial marching drums are displayed.

One painting (dated to 1751) shows the directors of the club gathered in the guildhall at the top table for an important meeting, dressed in smart coats and wigs.

The headquarters of the **Sint-Jorisgilde** (Guild of Crossbow Archers) is located in Stijn Streuvelstraat. The main room is somewhat smaller than the Longbow Guild's and has a beamed ceiling and tiled floor.

Portraits cover the walls here too, showing former guild members clutching their bows proudly. There is a fine collection of highly polished crossbows lined up against one wall, including one shaped like a rifle. Archery is still a fairly popular sport here even today.

A visit to the **Engelsklooster** (English Convent) on Carmerstraat comes alive when the tour guides show up. They are the nuns who live and worship here and they offer a fascinating insight into the convent.

It is an elegant baroque building, founded in 1629 and luxuriously designed in parts. It became famous for providing sanctuary and comfort for Catholics exiled from England. Its most noted guest was Charles II. The nuns will explain the different parts of the church and the remarkable marble altar.

At least 20 **windmills** once stood around the fortified outskirts of Bruges in the middle of the 16th century.

Sint-Sebastiaansgilde

Carmersstraat 174
☎ 33 16 26
🕐 Summer: Mon & Fri: 10am–12noon. Wed & Sat: 2pm–4pm. Tue, Thu, Sun: closed. Winter: Mon & Wed: 10am–12noon. Admission charge.

Sint-Jorisgilde

Stijn Streuvelstraat 59
☎ 34 24 01
🕐 Visits by appointment only.

Detail from Volkskundig boeket *by Le Flagais,* Museum voor Volkskunde

Schuttersgilde Sint Sebastiaan

Now just three remain, along the eastern stretch of the perimeter canal between Kruispoort and Dampoort. They are more recent.

Engelsklooster

Carmerstraat 85
☎ 33 24 28
🕐 Mon-Sun except first Sun in month: 9am-12noon, 2pm-5pm.
Admission free.

One of them, the **Sint-Janshuismolen**, is open to the public during the summer months. Paying it a visit is great fun. When there is a good wind behind the sails the whole mill rocks quite violently. You have to climb up a wide, steep, wooden ladder to get to the entrance which is about 16 metres (50 feet) off the ground. Once inside you realise the mill is a working museum. It still grinds grain, more than 200 years after it was first installed here in 1770.

You can inch round the workings on two levels as the wheels spin and the stones grind together. Despite creaking loudly and feeling as if it's about to topple over at any minute, the mill is sturdy.

Sint-Janshuismolen

Between Kruispoort and Dampoort on canal
☎ 45 21 11
🕐 May-Sep: Mon-Sun: 9.30am-12.30pm, 1.30pm-5pm.
Oct-Apr: closed.
Admission charge.
2 admissions for the price of 1 with voucher on page 69.

There is a collection of postcard-sized photographs stuck on to the wooden beams to explain the workings and the miller guides on duty are also helpful.

From the narrow balcony at the entrance, the view south towards the Kruispoort (Cross Gate, page 39) is good if you can stand still long enough to appreciate it. The queues waiting to climb into the windmill can be long on weekends in mid-summer and the miller guides take fixed lunch breaks, but it is well worth the wait.

The other two windmills along this stretch of the old city wall include the **Bonne**

Chiere (Good Show) which was built in 1888 and refurbished about 20 years later, and **De Niuewe Papegaii** (New Parrot) which has only been there for 30 years.

The **Museum Onze Lieve Vrouwe ter Potterie** (Museum of Our Lady of the Pottery) is located in a former hospital complex on Potterierei. The buildings date from between the 14th and 17th centuries. The collection inside includes art and sculptures by Bruges artists, furniture from the Gothic to the baroque eras, silverware and local tapestries. Part of the complex was once a church and has one of the city's most impressive baroque interiors.

Bruges would not be Bruges without a museum dedicated to one of its most famous exports – beer. The **Brouwerij Museum** (Brewery Museum) is in a former malthouse dating back to the start of the 20th century. There is a 400-year-old working brewery, De Gouden Boom, next door to the museum.

There is an entire section given over to the ancient art of the cooper, or barrel-maker, which shows in detail the whole process from beating out the metal hoops to measuring the wood panels, and finally putting the whole thing together.

Another part of the museum shows how the hops were added, and there are displays of brewery carts and bridles of the horses who pulled them. There is a corking machine (some beers were served from corked bottles), a collection of clogs and another of colourful posters advertising the brewery's various products, and a replica of an old bar with archery memorabilia on the walls and ceiling. Your ticket gets you a free drink at the end of the tour.

The **Kruispoort** (Cross Gate) is one of only four remaining gates that were put up to defend the wealthy Bruges from plunder. There were originally seven, all built in medieval times, and two are to the south of the city (page 31). Of the northerly gates, Kruispoort dates from 1402 and the **Ezelport** (Donkeys' Gate) that stands today in fact dates from the 17th and 18th centuries when it was rebuilt.

Museum Onze Lieve Vrouwe ter Potterie

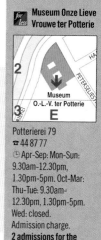

Potterierei 79
☎ 44 87 77
🕐 Apr-Sep: Mon-Sun: 9.30am-12.30pm, 1.30pm-5pm. Oct-Mar: Thu-Tue: 9.30am-12.30pm, 1.30pm-5pm. Wed: closed. Admission charge.
2 admissions for the price of 1 with voucher on page 71.

Brouwerij Museum

Verbrand Nieuwland 10
☎ 33 06 99
🕐 Apr-Sep: Wed-Sun: 2pm-6pm. Admission charge includes one drink.

Kruispoort

Ezelport

Beyond the City

Belgium's countryside is easily accessible by car, bicycle and public transport

If you want a day out of Bruges but don't want to trek too far, try the suburbs of Tillegembos and Loppem. You can reach them by car or bus, or even cycle if you have rented bicycles for your stay (some hotels provide them free).

Tillegembos is a wooded area situated south-west of the city. There are walking trails through the trees and around the lake, and play areas where children can be let loose. There is also a stately 14th-century chateau in the grounds which is worth a visit.

There is an even more impressive chateau, however, in the suburb of **Loppem**, 3km (2 miles) south of Bruges. It was designed in the mid 19th century by August Pugin, who also worked on much of the interior design of the British Houses of Parliament in London, under its architect Sir Charles Barry.

The chateau is immensely tall, climbing five or six storeys in places, and extremely elegant. It is somewhat reminiscent of a Scottish castle, but the mellow brick and Gothic roofs make it look at home here in continental Europe.

On windless days its reflection in the mirror-still lake is almost perfect, making it seem taller still. Inside it is full of antique furniture and the most luxurious

Reflections

"I'm not Caucasian, I'm Belgian" – Toots Thielemans, Belgian jazz musician upholstery and interior design.

Damme is a charming small town 7km (4 miles) north-east of Bruges and makes a good day out. Getting there is half the fun. You can walk all the way from the Jan van Eyckplein, north of the Markt, along Speigelrei and Lange Rei until you reach the Noorweegsekaai, then follow the poplar-shaded canal all the way. The canal goes eventually to **Sluis**, a small town just over the border in Holland and passes Damme en route. Or you could cycle. It must qualify as one of the most attractive rides in northern Europe, especially on a late spring day.

Damme was the main port here for many years after the river silted up and the harbour at Bruges ran dry. The small town resembles its larger cousin in miniature. There is an imposing **Stadhuis** dating from 1468 in a square in the centre of town; the **St. Janshospitaal**, records of which go back to the early part of the 13th century; and the **Onze Lieve Vrouwkerk** (Church of Our Lady).

The main street is full of good restaurants which serve a wide range of dishes and snacks, from home-made tomato soup and crusty bread to full steak meals. *(Tourist Information Office: Jakob van Maerlantstraat 3, ☎ (050) 35 33 19.)*

A windmill near Damme

Knokke is a small coastal resort on the North Sea, near the Dutch border. It is a genteel place, with elegant hotels along the seafront. Many wealthy Belgians have second homes here which they use at weekends and for summer holidays. *(Tourist Information Office: Zeedijk 660, ☎ (050) 63 03 80.)*

In the 19th century **Ostend** was a glamorous seaside resort known for its fresh, bracing air and healthy seafood. Infirm Europeans would trek here to sit on the promenade and "take the air". Although the glamour has faded, Ostend still makes an interesting day trip from Bruges.

The **promenade** has been widened and repaved in recent years to accommodate an increase in tourists. The **Casino**, which once, famously, welcomed the mighty American soul singer Marvin Gaye when he lived here briefly, now hosts regular classical concerts from touring orchestras.

The **James Ensorhuis** on Vlaanderenstraat is a small museum dedicated to the painter who once lived here. Ensor was one of the best known Belgian artists of the late 19th century. Many of his works followed the gruesome, dark themes of Hieronymus Bosch.

There is a large aquarium, the **Noordzeeaquarium**, but when it comes to fish in Ostend, most visitors would rather be eating them. Part of the town's draw is its food. Mussels and lobster are favourites, along with freshwater eels cooked in a green sauce much like the traditional eel shops in the East End of London. *(Tourist Information Office: Monacoplein, ☎ (059) 70 11 99.)*

Zeebrugge is a big North Sea port due north of Bruges. It is a main gateway for ferries to the UK as well as a busy harbour for international cargo. Many people remember

Ostend

Ostend

it as the site of the March 1987 disaster
when 193 people died as the roll-on roll-
off ferry *The Herald of Free Enterprise*
sank just out of port. The bow doors to
the car deck had not been closed properly
before departure. *(Tourist Information Office:*
☎ *(050) 54 50 42 (Jul and Aug only).)*

Bruges's big brother to the east, **Ghent,**
went through a similar commercial rise
and fall thanks to the cloth trade. After
the decline its new-found wealth came not
from tourism but heavy industry in the
19th century. This did little to preserve its
character and instead covered much of
the place in soot, but today Ghent still has
its picturesque corners.

The city can be a breath of fresh air after
sightseeing among the crowds in Bruges.
There is less of a scramble for café tables
and the queues to see attractions are
shorter.

Worth seeing is the dramatic Gothic
architecture of **St. Baafskathedraal** (St.
Baaf's Cathedral) in St. Baafsplein, the
Lakenhalle with its belfry which was the
former centre of the cloth trade here, and
the 12th-century **Het Gravensteen** castle
with its macabre torture chambers.

Also, take a walk along the **Graslei**, a
street by the harbour front which gives you
a view of well-preserved medieval guild

Ghent

Reflections

"In Flanders fields the poppies blow
Between the crosses, row on row
That mark our place; and in the sky
The larks, still bravely singing, fly
Scarce heard amid the guns below" – John McCrae, Canadian poet

houses. Down here by the water visitors will get a good sense of what dock life must have been like, especially if they come on a day when one of the North Sea's big storms is raging.

Much of Ghent has been refurbished in recent years with restoration work being carried out on ancient buildings and new ones rising as more business has been attracted into the city. *(Tourist Information Office: Stadhuis, ☎ (09) 266 5232.)*

It is hard to comprehend fully the massive loss of life in the First World War but a trip to the famous **battlegrounds** south-west of Bruges near the French border will certainly give visitors a good idea.

These are solemn fields, stretching away to the horizon. They have never lost their air of pain and death. After the Germans invaded Belgium and swept across the Flanders region, this is where they met the Allied forces head on. One battle alone, in 1917 near Passchendaele (now **Passendale**), caused the deaths of hundreds of thousands of soldiers.

Throughout this area are vast war cemeteries, including what is said to be the biggest one in the world at **Tyne Cot**. More than 150 are maintained by the Commonwealth War Graves Commission. They were originally laid out with military precision and are kept in excellent condition. Each one has row upon row of graves - a staggering number. Where the deceased's identity is known it is etched on the gravestone. Thousands are unmarked.

Organised tours of the cemeteries and other important wartime sites run from Ieper. Or you could pick up maps and guidebooks from Ieper (below) and head out on your own, either by car or bicycle. The land is fairly flat so the ride is not strenuous.

Ieper (Ypres), a small town near the French border, has found itself at the crossroads of history on more than one occasion. It was a key location during the height of the cloth industry, being strategically placed on the main trade route between Paris and Bruges. It got quite used to rival armies struggling for the territory around its perimeters.

Nothing, however, could have prepared it for the onslaught that the First World War brought to this corner of Belgium. The town was commandeered as the Allied troops' field base – the nearest to the front line. The German army shelled it relentlessly and the entire town was evacuated in 1915. By the time the Armistice message crackled through the radio on 11 November, 1918, the town was flattened. The medieval-style buildings that stand today are replicas of those that were destroyed.

War cemetery near Ieper

St. Maartenskathedraal (St. Martin's Cathedral) looks like its 13th-century original but is in fact only 70 years old. Unsurprisingly, it is dedicated to those who lost their lives in Flanders.

The **Ypres Salient Museum** is a good starting point for touring the town. It gives a blow by blow account of the war and the impact it had on the place and its people. The museum does not attempt to sanitize the horrors of war and so some of the photographs are gruesome and chilling but leave visitors with a powerful sense of reality. To cap the whole experience, each evening at 8pm a bugler sounds the Last Post at the Menin Gate near the Grote Markt. *(Tourist Information Office: Stadhuis, ☎ (057) 22 85 84.)*

Like Ieper, **Kortrijk**, which is only 7km (4 miles) from the French border, has seen its share of devastation over the years. It was hit by most of the conflicts that raged through this part of northern Europe. It probably did not help that it was also another key Flemish town in the medieval cloth trade, which no doubt provoked some resentment from the French.

One of the most famous disputes to occur here was the Battle of the Golden Spurs in July, 1302. A well-armed troop of mounted French knights was tricked by a rival army of Flemish cloth weavers, led by the revolutionary and Flemish hero Jan Breydel, whose statue stands in the Markt in Bruges.

Cloth Hall, Ieper

The weavers, with only crude weapons at their disposal, knew they could not win by force alone so covered an area of deep mud outside the town with foliage onto which the French knights rode, sank, and were massacred. It was a significant victory and to celebrate, the weavers tore spurs from the dead knights' boots as trophies, carried them back and laid them out on the floor of the nave of the **Onze Lieve Vrouwekerk** (Church of Our Lady) in the centre of town.

Antwerp city hall

The church is worth a visit to see some fine paintings, and there is also a museum of Flemish *objets d'art*, pottery, tiles and crafts. *(Tourist Information Office: Schouwburgplein 14, ☎ (056) 23 93 71.)*

Veurne is a small market town near the North Sea coast which is worth a brief stop for a look at the **Grote Markt** (Central Square) which is regarded by many as one of the best preserved in Belgium. *(Tourist Information Office: Grote Markt 29, ☎ (058) 33 05 31.)*

Belgium's second city, **Antwerp**, is a bustling, energetic place, with some handsome buildings. It grew rapidly in medieval times despite not being known as a cloth trade centre. Emperor Maximilian, after his humiliating experience being locked up by the authorities in Bruges when he was still heir to the Hapsburg throne, was determined to have his revenge and at every opportunity favoured Antwerp for trade and growth.

Tensions between Protestants and Catholics ran high here during the 16th century. Many fine buildings were destroyed and the economy all but collapsed.

Reflections

'As Antwerp goes, so goes the rest of Belgium a few years later' – Belgian saying

Grand Place, Brussels

Today, however, Antwerp is rebuilt and thriving as Belgium's largest port. It has recently undergone a refurbishment programme that has left many parts of the city with new buildings, cafés and restaurants.

The Flemish master painter Pieter Paul Rubens lived and worked in Antwerp from 1587. Many of his most famous works are scattered around the city, in churches, museums and in the building where he and his family lived, the **Rubenshuis**.

One part of the city has kept its dishevelled charm. Antwerp is the core of the world's diamond trade, a business which is run from grimy buildings around the Centraal Station. There is an air of mystery and intrigue about this part of the city, fuelled by the knowledge that behind some of these scruffy facades might be priceless precious stones.

The **Diamantmuseum** (Diamond Museum) on Lange Herentalsestraat is worth a quick tour as it gives a good introduction to the clandestine trade and shows the journey a diamond makes from mine to tiara. *(Tourist Information Office: Grote Markt 15,* ☎ *(03) 232 0103.)*

Situated about an hour's train ride south-east of Bruges, **Brussels** is the capital and biggest city in Belgium. It is a busy, modern, commercial and political centre, not just for its own country but for Europe. Many pan-European organizations

Reflections

"There was a sound of revelry by night, And Belgium's capital had gathered then Her beauty and her chivalry, and bright The lamps that shone o'er fair women and brave men" – Lord Byron, *Childe Harold's Pilgrimage*

are based here, including the European Commission and Nato.

The city also offers a wealth of museums, churches, restaurants, cafés and monuments such as the **Manneken-Pis**, the world famous fountain statue of a small naked boy urinating. Throughout the year the child is dressed in different costumes to mark certain occasions.

The **Grand Place** (Main Square) is one of the finest city squares in Europe, with elegant guildhouses around the perimeter (a reminder of the wealth on which Brussels was built) and smart cafés spreading out over the cobblestones.

Flemish and French have equal status here, despite the fact that Brussels is located in the French-speaking part of the country. All the streets are named in both languages. However, as this is a major crossroads of Europe, English is widely spoken by almost everyone. *(Office de Tourisme et d'Information de Bruxelles (TIB): Hôtel de Ville, Grand Place, ☎ (02) 513 8940; Maison de Tourisme, rue Marché aux Herbes 63, ☎ (02) 504 0390.)*

Day trips to **France** from Bruges are possible. The border is just over an hour's drive away, with the cities of **Lille**, **Roubaix** and **Lens** just a little beyond that.

There are high-speed train services, which offer great value for money, between **Paris** and **Brussels** and slower routes from Bruges to **Lille**, some via Ghent. Information about services and prices can be had from the main railway stations.

The Eiffel Tower, Paris

Dining

Bruges has a wide range of good restaurants. It is easy to avoid those which are specifically geared towards tourists, and therefore charge higher prices. Some suggestions are made in the margins.

The cafés around the Markt all offer vast tureens of steaming **Moules frites** (mussels and French fries). The mussels are cooked in butter and garlic and sometimes herbs such as fennel are used to add flavour. A bowl makes the perfect lunchtime snack, washed down with a light **witbeer** or a glass of white wine.

But first, breakfast; expect Flemish hotel breakfasts to offer cold meats and cheese with rolls rather than the French equivalent of croissants and coffee, although this is also available in some establishments. A good Bruges breakfast can fill you up until after the worst of the lunchtime rush.

Living in a northern city where the winter temperatures can often drop below freezing as Arctic winds blast down across the North Sea, the chefs of Bruges have concocted some warming dishes over the generations.

A favourite first course is **escargots bourguignonne**. Snails are roasted in garlic and served with crusty bread. The standard size is a plate of about 25 snails which can be a bit much for a starter but most restaurants will do smaller portions.

A good main course to chase away the chill or revive the spirit after a morning sightseeing is Flemish **cod**. In most restaurants you will be served a huge portion of fish which has been cooked in butter with herbs, potatoes and tomatoes, almost like a light fish stew.

Lobsters and **oysters** are common, usually caught the night before and brought straight from the fishing towns along the North Sea coast.

For meat lovers there are some satisfying game stews to try. **Rabbit** is popular with the people of Bruges, as are game birds like **partridge** and **quail**. Winter visitors

Spinola
Flemish / Seafood

Spinolarei 1
☎ 34 17 85
🕐 Tue-Sat: lunch and dinner. Sun-Mon: closed.

Den Dyver
Flemish

Dijver 5
☎ 33 60 69
🕐 Fri-Tue: lunch and dinner. Wed-Thu: closed.

't Mozarthuys
Bistro

Huidenvettersplein 1

might be able to find **hotpots**, stews of vegetables and meat which often include various unrecognisable bits of offal. Year round a mainstay of the Belgian diet is *waterzooi* – a clear soup with fish or chicken.

Vegetarians will have a harder time as most Flemish food is based on meat or fish, but if you look hard enough you can find places that do good vegetable soups and salads.

Some restaurants have the same menus for lunch and evening meals. Getting into the habit of eating bigger meals at midday allows more time to sample the many and varied beers (see *Nightlife*, page 54) in the evening after a light snack.

Prices are generally fairly reasonable and people tend to eat early in the evening (another northern European trait). Eating out in Bruges is certainly cheaper than in Brussels where even the most simple of meals can be expensive.

Belgium is famous for its chocolate which is reputed to be the finest in the world. Throughout the city, but especially around the Markt and the Burg, there are several shops selling all kinds of **chocolate** in a wide variety of shapes. You can buy a standard crate of mixed flavoured centres or an individually wrapped single praline that comes in a tiny box.

Duc de Bourgogne
Luxury

Huidenvettersplein 12
☎ 33 20 38

Open-air dining in central Bruges

Shopping

On the surface, Bruges's shopping scene is geared towards tourists, but there is actually a good range of shops and stores selling things other than gifts and souvenirs.

Prices compare with other smaller European cities but are slightly cheaper than major capitals like Brussels, London or Paris. If you are from outside the European Union, look out for the shops that have Duty Free signs in the window as their prices will be cheaper still.

A display of traditional Bruges lace

For general shops head for **Steenstraat**, the street that leads south-west off the Markt. Here you will find most of the brand names in clothes and home furnishings. A large market is held every Saturday at **t'Zand**, at the end.

Steenstraat

Also in Steenstraat, near the entrance to the Markt, is a shop devoted to the Belgian cartoon hero Tintin and his pals. The character was created by an illustrator from Brussels known as Hergé (but whose real name was Georges Rémi). The shop sells anything from keyrings to postcards, children's mobiles to footballs, T-shirts to schoolbags, and of course the famous picture books themselves.

t'Zand

🕐 Market: Sat: 7am–1pm.

The chances are that you'll want to take home a traditional Bruges-style souvenir. A favourite gift to bring back from Belgium is chocolate and there is lots to buy in the city. In the streets leading off the Markt there are shops selling slabs of it. You can buy pieces in pre-packaged cartons or get very expensive individual truffles wrapped in rice paper and nestled in delicate pink boxes tied up with bows.

Another typical souvenir is an attractively

bottled Belgian beer. Many shops and supermarkets sell beer at reasonable prices, offering a good opportunity to stock up on some rarer labels.

The cloth trade made Bruges a wealthy commercial centre and although that trade has turned to tourism now and left the spinning and weaving behind, high quality lace is still made here and commands a high price.

It is best to shop around and ask at the tourism information centre for a list of lace shops. The **Kantcentrum** (Lace Centre, page 35) on Peperstraat is another place that should be able to advise. Exquisite tapestries are also available from certain shops.

One of the joys of shopping in Bruges is the markets, and the **flea market** on the Dijver is a must. The stall-holders sell a bizarre range of goods. The bigger items often include huge clay chimney pots, heavy cast-iron shoe-scrapers, and brass doorknockers in the shape of roaring lions, while the smaller tables display jewellery, trinket boxes, pipes, china mugs, Victorian umbrellas, slender camera tripods and piles of old books, magazines and maps of Flanders. It is certainly worth a discussion over the price although the stall-holders are not really prepared to haggle.

There might be some bargain antiques and paintings on the stalls of Bruges's flea markets but it is more likely such goods will be displayed in one of the city's more exclusive and expensive boutiques. Before buying an antique of any sort check it is legal to export it and that all the paperwork has been signed so you can bring it back to your country.

Kantcentrum

Peperstraat 3a
☎ 33 00 72

Flea market

Dijver
🕐 Mar-Oct: Sat-Sun: afternoons only.

A tapestry shop

Nightlife

Bruges is not known for its nightlife. There are only one or two small music venues and no nightclubs. In fact it was probably considerably wilder in medieval times than it is now.

What it does have in abundance, however, is a host of welcoming bars and cafés serving coffee, snacks and hundreds of different types of beer.

Belgian beer is among the most celebrated in the world and for good reason. This tiny country produces what must be the widest variety of beers. In most Bruges bars you will be handed a menu when you walk in – for beer, not food.

There are light, crystal-clear, blond or amber ones, refreshing and crisp. The white beers are brewed with wheat and are distinctive for their cloudy appearance.

Lambic beers are organic in the sense that during fermentation they are exposed to wild yeast. They can be sharp on the tongue and are more of an acquired taste but many are sweetened with fruit flavourings. Cherry and strawberry beers are very popular.

A lot of Belgian beers were originally brewed by monks in monasteries dotted throughout the country. This is why today many bottles have labels showing the monks at work on their brews. Some labels are quite irreverent and depict the friars incapable after sampling too much of their concoctions.

Among the most popular are *Orval*, a dark beer which comes from a monastery in the south of the country; *Rochefort* from Namur (central southern Belgium) which has a variety with 11 per cent alcohol that tastes like alcoholic drinking chocolate; *Hoegaarden*, a light and refreshing *witbee* which is nice with a squeeze of lemon juice; and *Trappist Leffe*, a strong, dark beer with a sweet aftertaste.

Each brewery not only produces its own beers but delivers them in uniquely shaped bottles and provides bars with individual designs of glass in which to

Brouwerij Taverne
Bar

Walplein 26
☎ 33 26 97

Café Brugs Beertje
Bar

Kemelstraat 5
☎ 33 96 16
🕑 Closed Wed.

Craenenburg café

Markt 16
☎ 33 34 02
🕑 Mon-Fri, Sun: 7.30am-
11pm. Sat: 7.30am-1am.

serve them. The glasses are on sale in many bars and from the breweries themselves.

Not all bars serve food as well, but you can get a plate of cold meats, bread, cheese and pickles to pick at while you drink. It will help soak up some of the alcohol.

One bar to try for its extensive range of beers is the

Bruges illuminated at night

Café Brugs Beertje on Kemelstraat. It is a cosy, friendly place, with wooden tables and lots of conversation. There are more than 300 beers to choose from, all catalogued in a hefty menu. The plate of meat and cheese is excellent.

If it is a late night coffee you are after then try any of the cafés in the Markt. The **Craenenburg** is the most famous but all are good. After dinner on a warm evening it is nice to sit out here and admire the Belfort bathed in orange light.

For a night at the cinema, head for Zilverstraat, where there are two. Most films are shown in their original language, and the layers of French and Dutch subtitles can be rather offputting and take up half the screen.

Annual festivals provide welcome boosts to Bruges's nightlife. The Festival of the Canals every August features a pageant and illuminations along the waterways. There is a film festival in March, with an eclectic selection of films being shown at various venues.

For information about films, festivals and other night-time entertainments, contact the Tourist Information Centre (page 14). Here you can pick up free events guides such as *Agenda Brugge* and *Exit Light*.

Zilverstraat

Bruges Tourism Information and Reservation Centre

11 Burg
☎ 44 86 86
🕐 Apr-Sep: Mon-Fri: 9.30am-6.30pm. Sat-Sun: 10am-12noon, 2pm-6.30pm. Oct-Mar: Mon-Fri: 9.30am-5pm. Sat: 9.30am-12.45pm, 2pm-5pm. Sun: closed.

Visitor Information

A café on Wijngaardplein

CHILDREN

As the number one tourist destination in Belgium, it is hardly surprising that children are well catered for. There are a number of museums and attractions of specific interest to children, as well as distractions that all the family will enjoy.

Kids love climbing the **Belfort** tower (page 11) and seeing the city from its impressive height. It is also fun allowing children to lead you through the picturesque maze of alleys in **Steenstraat**. One street that should not be missed is **Stoofstraat**, the narrowest street in the whole city.

The swans on **Minnewater** (page 29) make interesting viewing for younger children, while their older siblings will be fascinated by the backdrop of the old city walls and the round towers of **Gentpoort** (page 31).

Sint Michiels, south of Bruges is the location of the **Boudewijnpark** (☎ *050 38 38 38*), a must if you have children of different ages to keep amused. Not only does it have one of the most spectacular dolphin aquaria in Europe, it also caters specifically for small children in its Bambinoland, and offers more than 30 different attractions and rides throughout the park.

Further afield is the seaside resort of

ELECTRIC CURRENT

Electricity in Belgium runs on 220V with a two-pin plug.

Ostend (page 42), which is less crowded and calmer than Bruges. There is a large aquarium and a good selection of restaurants selling fresh fish and chips.

CUSTOMS

Import restrictions for persons travelling from outside the EU are: **Tobacco**: 200 cigarettes; **Alcohol**: 2 litres of wine plus 1 litre of spirits.

Import restrictions for EU residents are: **Tobacco**: 800 cigarettes; **Alcohol**: 90 litres of wine plus 10 litres of spirits.

EVENTS / FESTIVALS

There are a number of religious and secular celebrations held throughout the year in Belgium. Dates change each year, so for an up-to-date listing contact the national tourist office in your home country or in Bruges upon your arrival.

The most famous religious event in Bruges is the *Heilig Bloedprocessie* (Procession of the Holy Blood) held 40 days after Easter each year (page 16).

HEALTH AND SAFETY

EU residents are entitled to emergency health services enjoyed by Belgians on the state system. As this does not cover all medical situations, both EU and non-EU nationals are advised to take out comprehensive travel insurance which includes medical coverage.

EMERGENCIES

Emergency telephone numbers are ☎ 100 for an ambulance or the fire service and ☎ 101 for the police.

A display of delicious seafood

Sightseeing by horse-drawn cab

For the treatment of minor ailments, go to a pharmacy. These are recognizable by a green cross, and some are open 24 hours a day. A list of pharmacies open around the clock is available from the Tourist Information Office. Pharmacy windows also display duty rotas.

The crime rate in Belgium is one of the lowest in Europe. That said, it is advisable to take the usual precautions against pickpockets. Always leave the bulk of your money in the hotel safe, take a copy of your travel documents and passport, and keep valuables out of sight.

If you are robbed, you will need to contact the police. They will then issue a report with a number that you should make a note of. You will need this number when making an insurance claim. The main police station is at Hauwerstraat 7, ☎ 44 88 44. Most police officers on the street speak some English.

LEFT LUGGAGE

There are left luggage lockers at the train station that can be accessed between 5am and midnight. There are also lockers at the Tourist Information Centre.

HOTELS

Below is a selection of hotels for various budgets in or near the centre of Bruges, where 🛠 = 1,000BF for a standard double room per night. If you would rather take your chances, bear in mind that although there are over one hundred sleeping establishments, places are quickly booked up in the popular summer months. Most of the more expensive hotels are found south of the Burg, while more reasonable places are near the Spiegelrei canal or around the cathedral.

De Tuilerieen *(Dijver 7, ☎ 34 36 91.)* 💰 💰 💰 💰 💰

Parkhotel *(Vrijdagmarkt 5, ☎ 33 33 64.)* 💰 💰 💰 💰

Duc de Bourgogne *(Huidenvettersplein 12, ☎ 33 20 38.)* 💰 💰 💰 💰 💰

Egmond *(Minnewater 15, ☎ 34 14 45.)* 💰 💰 💰 💰

Bourgoensche Cruyce *(Wollestraat 41-43, ☎ 33 79 26.)* 💰 💰 💰 💰

Hostellerie Pannenhuis *(Zandstraat 2, ☎ 31 19 07.)* 💰 💰 💰 💰

't Speelmanshuys *('t Zand 3, ☎ 33 95 52.)* 💰 💰

Kasteel Cateline *(Zandstraat 272, ☎ 31 70 26.)* 💰 💰 💰

Central *(Markt 30, ☎ 33 18 05.)* 💰 💰

Passage Budget Hotel *(Dweerstraat 26-28, ☎ 34 02 32.)* 💰 💰

LANGUAGE

In Belgium both French and Flemish are spoken. Flemish is spoken throughout Flanders in the north, although Flemish-speakers have equal language rights in Brussels, where the majority speak a French dialect known as Walloon.

The English language is also widely spoken, especially in the tourist trade and most hotels. Learning a few words of Flemish is always well received, although quite difficult to pronounce.

Hello	*Hallo / Dag*
Goodbye	*Tot ziens!*
Yes / No	*Ja / Nee*
Thank you	*Dank u wel*
Please	*Alstublieft*
Do you speak English?	*Spreekt u Engels?*
I don't understand	*Ik begrijp het nier*
I would like...	*Heeft u...*
Where is...	*Waar is...?*

MAIL / POST

Post offices open from 9am-4pm, Monday to Friday. The **central post office,** located at Markt 5, is also open on Saturdays from 9am-12noon. Post Restante letters can be sent to any major post office. Post boxes are red.

How much is it?	*Wat kost...?*
See you later	*Tot straks*
Open	*Open*
Closed	*Gesloten*
Post office	*Postkantoor*
Money exchange	*Wisselkantoor*

MONEY

The Belgian franc (BF) comes in denominations of 100, 200, 500, 1,000, 5,000 and 10,000BF notes, and coins of 1, 5, 20 and 50BF.

Banks and bureau de change invariably charge commission to change money. Banks are generally open 9am-4pm, Monday to Friday.

Outside these hours visitors with money to change should head for the exchange desk in the tourist office (⏱ Apr-Sep: Mon-Fri: 9.30am-6.30pm. Sat-Sun: 10am-6.30pm. Oct: Mon-Sun: 10am-5.30pm. Nov-Mar: Sat-Sun: 9.30am-5.30pm.)

International credit and debit cards can be used in bank machines. Major credit cards are accepted at establishments throughout the city.

Most large establishments in the centre of Brussels accept travellers' cheques, although the exchange rate might be quite high.

OPENING HOURS

Banks – Standard opening hours are 9am to 4pm Monday to Friday. Some close for an hour at lunchtime.

Bars / Restaurants – Many restaurants open just 6 days a week, closing on Monday or Tuesday. Some close as early as 10pm, but there are plenty of bars and cafés which are open into the early hours.

Museums / Galleries – This guide lists individual opening times under each museum's entry.

Shops – Business hours are generally 10am-6pm Monday to Saturday, and all but the very tourist-orientated establishments are closed on Sundays.

PACKING

Belgium has a temperate climate. Take heavy coats in the winter and a jumper for evenings even in midsummer. Take something waterproof all year round.
Many of the streets are cobbled, so it is wise to take comfortable, flat footwear as opposed to high-heeled shoes.

SPECIAL TRAVELLERS

Disabled travellers – Belgium has been slow to provide access and facilities for disabled people, and Bruges in particular, with its cobbled streets, is hard to negoiate. For general advice, contact the **Vlaamse Federatie voor Gehandicapten** *(32-38 rue St Jean, 1000 Bruxelles, ☎ (02) 515 0260.)*

A view of the Onze Lieve Vrouwekerk

Elderly – Concessions are available with proof of age. Where specified in this guide, *for less* discounts are available on top of the normal senior discount.

Students – Concessions are available at many attractions and museums when acceptable ID, such as an ISIC card, is produced. Where specified in this guide, *for less* discounts are available on top of the normal student discount.

Gay/lesbian – The gay and lesbian scene is not nearly as up-front as in many other countries, Amsterdam being a nearby example. There are gay clubs and bars, however, as well as periodicals serving the gay community. Try **Ravel** *(Karel de Stoutelaan 172, ☎ 31 52 74)* or **Lesbian Talking Bar** *('s Gravenstraat 44. ⏲ Thu only.)*

TELEPHONES

There is invariably a drastic mark-up on telephone calls made from hotels. Much cheaper are the public phones found at regular intervals throughout the city.

Public phones accept coins or telecards, which can be bought at post offices, news stands and supermarkets. Phones are also being adapted to accept credit cards.

TOURS

Interesting and entertaining day-long tours by minibus are run by **Quasimodo Tours** *(Leenhofweg 7, ☎ 37 04 70).* The circuit of

TELEPHONE CODES

The country code for Belgium is ☎ 32.

The code for Bruges is ☎ 050, which must be added when making calls from outside the city.

the First World War battlefields outside Ieper runs three times a week from April to October.

There are also walking or cycling tours of the city and its environs during the summer months. Details can be found at the Tourist Information Centre.

TOURIST INFORMATION / LISTINGS

Bruges Tourism Information and Reservation Centre

11 Burg
☎ 44 86 86
🕐 Apr-Sep: Mon-Fri: 9.30am-6.30pm. Sat-Sun: 10am-12noon, 2pm-6.30pm. Oct-Mar: Mon-Fri: 9.30am-5pm. Sat-Sun: 9.30am-12.45pm, 2pm-5pm.

There are two offices of **Toerisme Brugge**, one at the main entrance to the train station and one in Burg square, in the heart of Bruges. Their multi-lingual staff are on hand to answer any of your questions. You can also make hotel bookings free of charge, by leaving a deposit that is then deducted from your final hotel bill.

At the Tourist Information Centre you can also change currency, buy city maps and even book tickets for some of the city's shows and performances. There are bus timetables pinned up outside the entrance.

TRANSPORT TO BRUGES

By air – The closest airport to Bruges is Brussels Nationaal. It is easiest to continue your inward journey by train, as it takes only 90 minutes. You will need to change trains at Brussels North (alight at Brussels Central if you intend to do some sightseeing in Brussels first).

By road – The N9 via Ghent is the most direct and speedy route into the city. For

Eighteenth-century almshouses

those bringing a car by ferry, it is worth knowing that Bruges is only 90 minutes from Calais by motorway.

By rail – Eurostar from London Waterloo has made getting to Bruges easier than ever. The Eurostar reaches Brussels in just 3 hours 15 minutes, followed by another hour's journey with a connecting train to reach Bruges.

TRANSPORT AROUND THE CITY

Bus – The information kiosk outside the train station (☎ *35 54 51, ◷ Mon-Fri: 7.30am-6pm. Sat: 9am-6pm. Sun: 10am-6pm)* can answer all your queries about city and regional bus options. There are also timetables outside the tourist office.

It is possible to take a multi-lingual bus tour of the city to get your bearings in relation to the key sites. These leave from the Markt and last for just under an hour. The frequency of departure varies according to the season so contact the Tourist Information Centre for the latest details.

Car – Parking is considered something of a problem in Bruges, as in many other popular tourist cities. It is very expensive to use the limited street parking and very few hotels have any parking facilities. That said, there are five car parks in the city centre, with a total capacity of 2,405.

In addition, there are some free car parks along the ring road within walking distance of the city centre. Alternatively, if you park at the car park at the train station at a special rate, on presentation of your parking ticket you are entitled to free bus travel to and from the city centre.

Bruges has a healthy concern for the environment, and a traffic circulation plan has been introduced to discourage the use of cars in the city centre and safeguard the clean urban atmosphere. As part of this plan, many of the main streets are one-way and the overall speed limit is 30km/h (19 mp/h).

If you want to hire a car, contact **Europe Car** *(St. Pieterskaai 48, ☎ 31 45 44)* or **Hertz** *Baron Ruzettelaan 6, ☎ 37 36 71).*

TIPPING

Restaurants – Service is normally included in restaurant bills, although many people add an extra 5-10%.

Taxis – Taxi drivers do not necessarily expect a tip on top of their fare. Rounding up fares in taxis is appropriate if they have been particularly helpful.

Bicycles – Bruges is undeniably a cyclist's city, as is most evident by the flurry of commuter bikes at peak hours in the morning and evening. That cycling is encouraged is evident from the fact that on more than 50 city-centre streets that are one-way for cars, cyclists can travel in both directions.

For those who did not bring their own bicycles or who want to try their hand at cycling with a friend, bikes and tandems can be hired from the train station, from **Popelier** *(Mariastraat 26, ☎ 34 32 62)* or **'t Koffieboontje** *(Hallestraat 4, ☎ 33 80 27)*.

For an organized taster of Bruges by bike, join one of the fun guided tours run by the **Back Road Bike Company** *(☎ 37 04 70)*. It offers tours of the villages around Bruges and Damme on mountain bikes, lasting two or three hours and covering up to 30 km (17 miles).

Boat – Boats depart from many of the jetties south of the Burg, every day from March to November. The 30-minute tour of the city's central canals is held in at least three different languages The trips are hugely popular, so despite the regular departures queues tend to build up. Between December and February the service is drastically reduced, with weekend trips only.

If you fancy a boat trip out of town, then one possibility is an outing to Damme, which takes just over 40 minutes. Boats leave from the Noorweegsekaai – 2 km (1.2 miles) north of the city centre – five times a day between April and September.

Horse-drawn cab – Another popular tourist option is a horse-drawn cab tour starting from the Burg.

Taxis – There are taxi ranks at the **Markt** *(☎ 33 44 44)* and the **Stationsplein** *(☎ 38 46 60)*.

On foot – Bruges is the perfect city to tackle on foot. It is compact and most of the major sights are concentrated within a small area. You will find a good range of Belgian walking maps at **Brugse Boekhandel** at Dijver 2, situated at the bottom of Wollerstraat.

VISAS

EU nationals and those from Canada, the USA, Australia and New Zealand need only a valid passport for stays of up to three months. For longer stays, EU nationals need to register with the police who in return will issue a residency card that is valid for three months in the first instance, but can be renewed. Residence permits and work permits for non-EU nationals are much more difficult to acquire, and need to be applied for from the country of origin.

Alternatively, there are guided walking tours of the city centre, led by well-trained, professional guides who will fascinate you with insider stories of Bruges and historical details. You can find the latest details and times from staff at the tourist office.

USEFUL TELEPHONE NUMBERS

Airport information – ☎ *(02) 753 3211*

Ambulance/Fire – ☎ *100*

Area code – ☎ *(0)50*

Bus information line – ☎ *35 54 51*

Operator assistance / reverse charges – ☎ *1224*

Directory enquiries – ☎ *1207* (domestic), ☎ *1204* (international)

Police – ☎ *101*

Rail information – ☎ *38 23 82*

Tourist office – ☎ *44 86 86*

Weekend doctors – ☎ *81 38 99*

WOMEN TRAVELLERS

Women travelling alone in Belgium are unlikely to encounter any problems. That said, precautions should be taken in certain parts of the cities, as anywhere else in the world. Common sense should be adequate protection in most situations.

Wear a money belt around your waist instead of carrying a handbag on your shoulder, and don't keep wallets or money in pockets that are easily accessed by wandering fingers. Cars should not have any tempting items left visible and always lock your bicycle to something.

CREDITS

Principal photography: Photobank, Toerisme Brugge, Stad Brugge

Windowboxes

Index